T0130465

WELCOME TO CHESS!

Where Visual Spatial Learning activates your Metacognition!

"Think Before You Move"
By Phil Rosado

Mind Matter

AuthorHouse™
1663 Liberty Drive
Bloomington, IN 47403
www.authorhouse.com
Phone: 833-262-8899

This book is printed on acid-free paper.

Interior Image Credit: Eric Rosado

ISBN: 979-8-8230-0611-8 (sc)
ISBN: 979-8-8230-0610-1 (e)

Library of Congress Control Number: 2023906902

Print information available on the last page.

Published by AuthorHouse 04/18/2023

authorHOUSE®

Acknowledgements

I would like to acknowledge Dr. Hodge (R.I.P) former Principal of The Frederick Douglass Academy New York City Board of Education for appointing me to building a Chess club at The Frederick Douglass Academy, building a Chess team, and as a teacher of Chess as a class. At the same time, I would like to give thanks to Chess in the Schools - Director Ron Boocock and former instructor Eric Hutchins for their collaboration as our partners in forming Chess classes, creating a Chess club, and a Chess team and the coaches Joel Yofi and Jeff Kelleher. I would also like to give a "Shout Out" to our first team at FDA who took that journey as well.

I would also like to thank Marcos Bausch my former Principal at John Ericsson Middle School 126 for allowing me to build a Chess club, team, and teach Chess as a class as well. My thanks go to Chess in the Schools once more for their partnership at MS 126 as well. I would also like to give a "Shout Out" to our first team at MS 126 who continued that journey with me as well.

Cognitive Process in Chess

- The formula for deciding on a move: 1) We need to scan the board and the position of pieces Visually/Spatially to be viewed from both sides of the board. Therefore, you will see what categories of moves are available altogether for both sides of the board. 2) Now begin to develop a collection of moves that are available strategically. 3) Decision making is in having a Theory – a system of ideas and observations that are related to each other to justify the decision of the move selected. This concludes our three-step process in determining the theory of the move that can be executed. Whenever we ignore this three-step process that concludes the theories to be evaluated, we are most likely going to commit a blunder. The blunder is a move decided on based on an impulse usually followed by a saying "I didn't see that!" which involved no thought process. Now, there are really two adversaries, your opponent and yourself in activating the three steps needed to conclude a move.

- We begin with a review of the concept of thoughts metacognitively by using the selection of moves available like capture, protect, and run/retreat. This practice of the Pawn Race matches shows how the goal of advancement is achieved through positioning and teamwork, so Visual Spatial process needs to be implemented. The categories of moves like capture, protect, run/retreat is also applied in the Face-Off matches before making any decision in executing a move. This application of thought process begins and continues by using these categories of moves as an important tool for continuous thought practice to complete the outcome of capturing free and/or higher value material to reach its goal. A blunder is making a move in Chess that ends up in loss of material (pieces) and/or checkmate. This is usually caused when the metacognitive process is not practiced and/or is not consistent.

- This metacognitive process helps to understand how this practice is needed for the 3 stages of the game, 1) Opening to set up the foundation in development of material for control of the center squares, for the 2) Middle game for advancement in improving Positioning to transition towards the 3) End game for Positioning of possible Checkmate as well as how to stop advancement of possible Checkmate from opponent.

- Visual-Spatial learning helps you to perceive the visual information in the environment (chess board and pieces), to represent it internally, to integrate it with other senses and experiences, to derive meaning and understanding, and to perform manipulations and transformations on those perceptions (developing the material for advancement to the opponent's territory by creating passages by capturing material and/or landing on squares to be in Position for possible checkmate as well as preventing checkmate). It is the first language of the brain.

- Through Visual-Spatial learning in Chess you can explore and manipulate three-dimensional materials, developing and practicing many different skills simultaneously (e.g., construction, engineering, kinesthetic, math, literacy, social skills). You are also communicating the knowledge of the world, and learning to communicate, process, and manage emotions. Visual Spatial work is a language. Through building you can practice abstract thinking (Metacognition thought processing) in a concrete medium (chess board).

White territory 1 - 4 vs Black territory 8 - 5

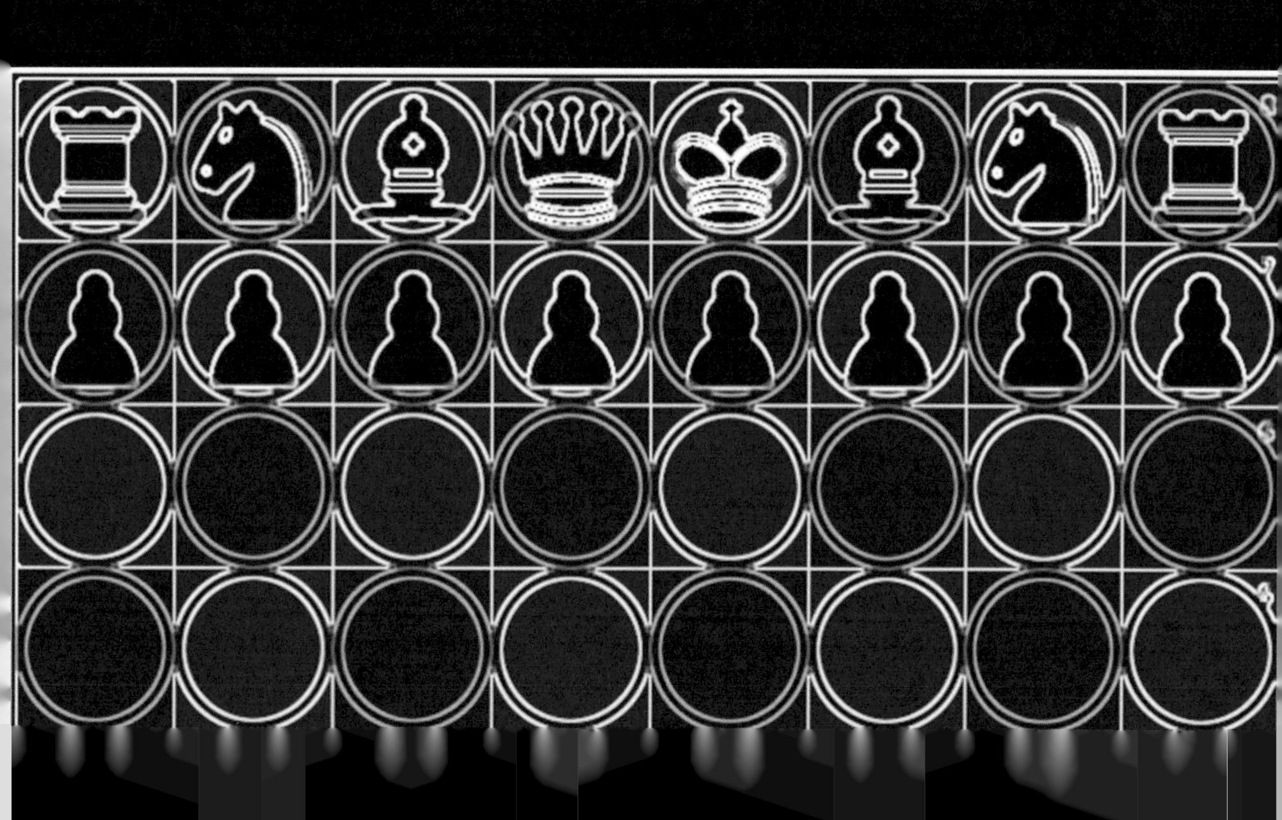

Chess board is made up of Files and Ranks

Files – elevators a thru h

Ranks –floors 1 thru 8

Pawn Race

- **Object of the Game in Pawn Race – Advancement, first Pawn to advance to other side of the Board safely without being Captured Wins!**

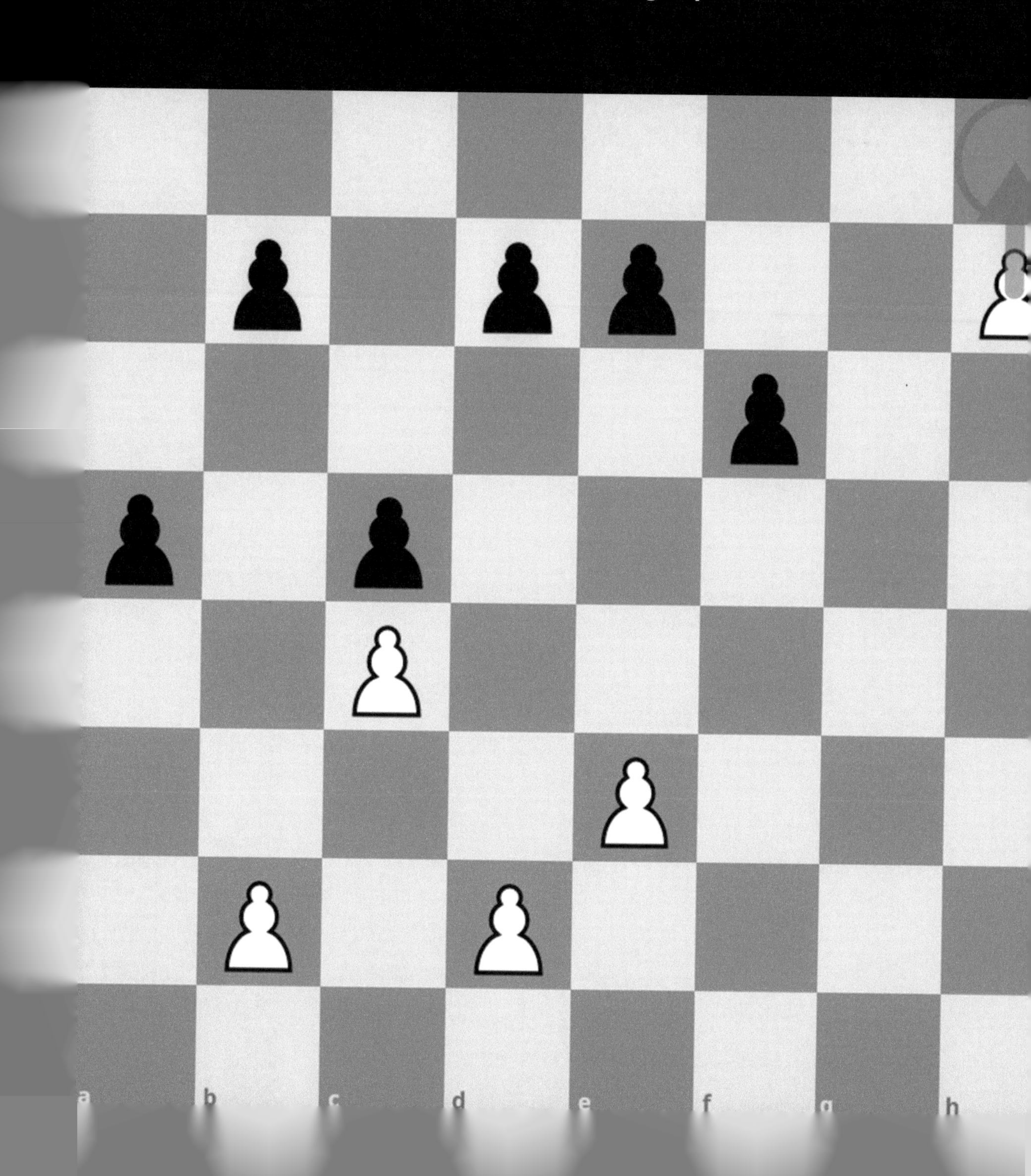

Pawns

- Pawns only move **Forward.** They never go backwards or sideways.
- **Pawns only move one square at a time EXCEPT** when they are on the starting rank, they have a choice to move one or two squares forward.
- **Pawns only Capture Diagonally.** Pawns can only Capture one square away diagonally and forward on the same color square.

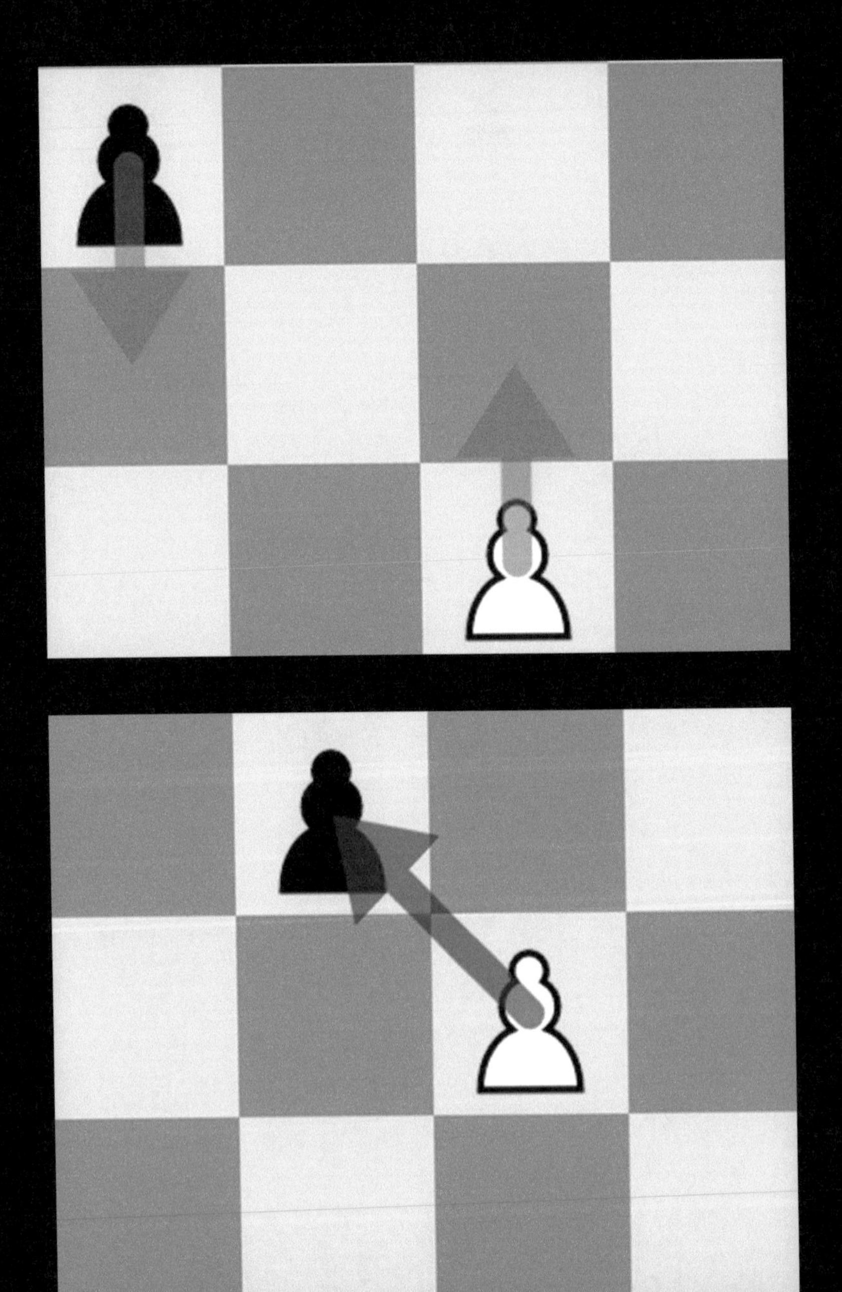

Pawn Race

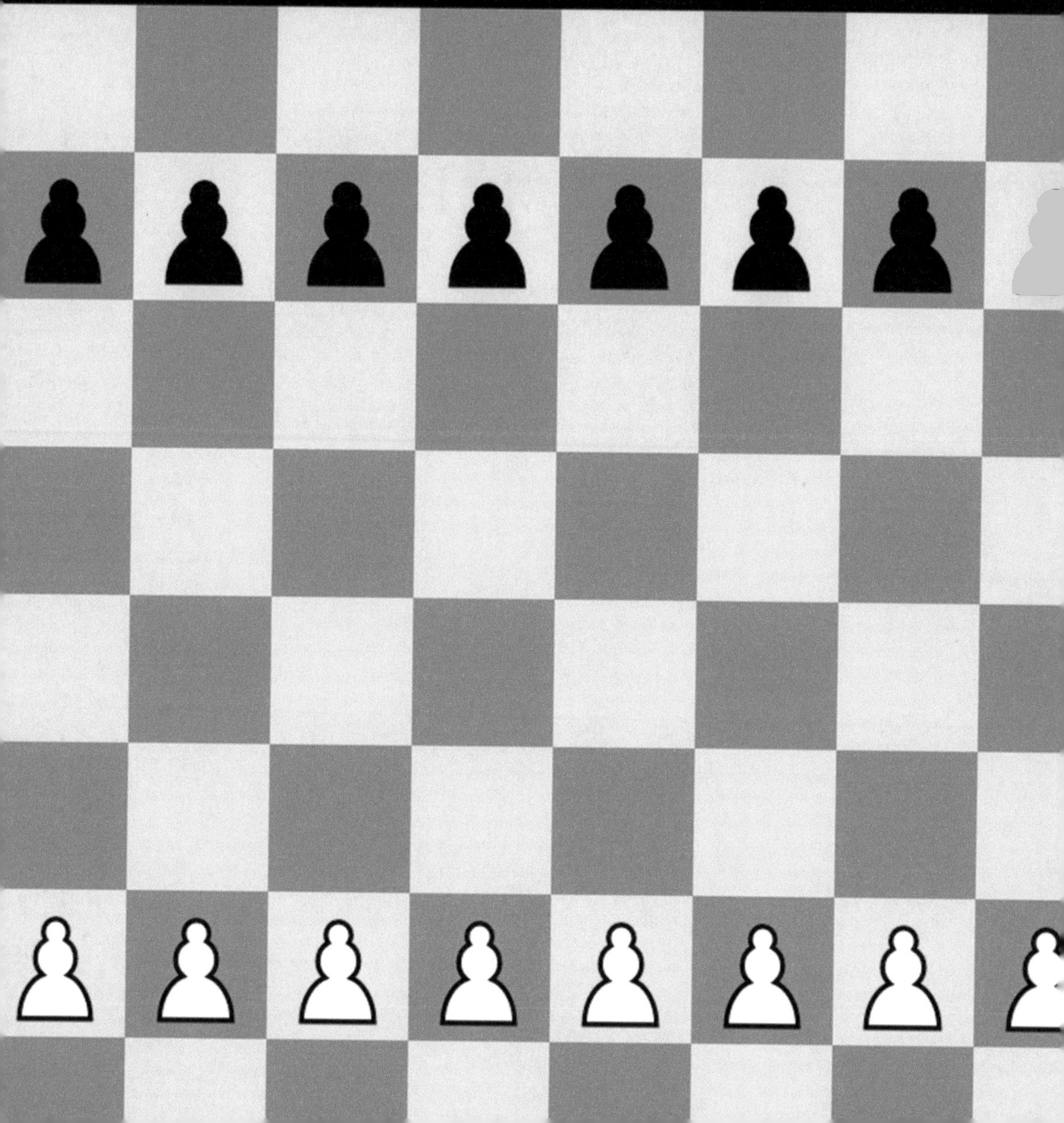

Face - off

hts and Rooks Face-Off against each other. After se
it more challenging by removing one Rook from play

Game is to try to Capture as many Pieces as possible wit

'rise" a Piece that is exposed to Capture for Free.

Higher Value in a Trade, even though you get captur
exchange where you get ahead in the outcome with a

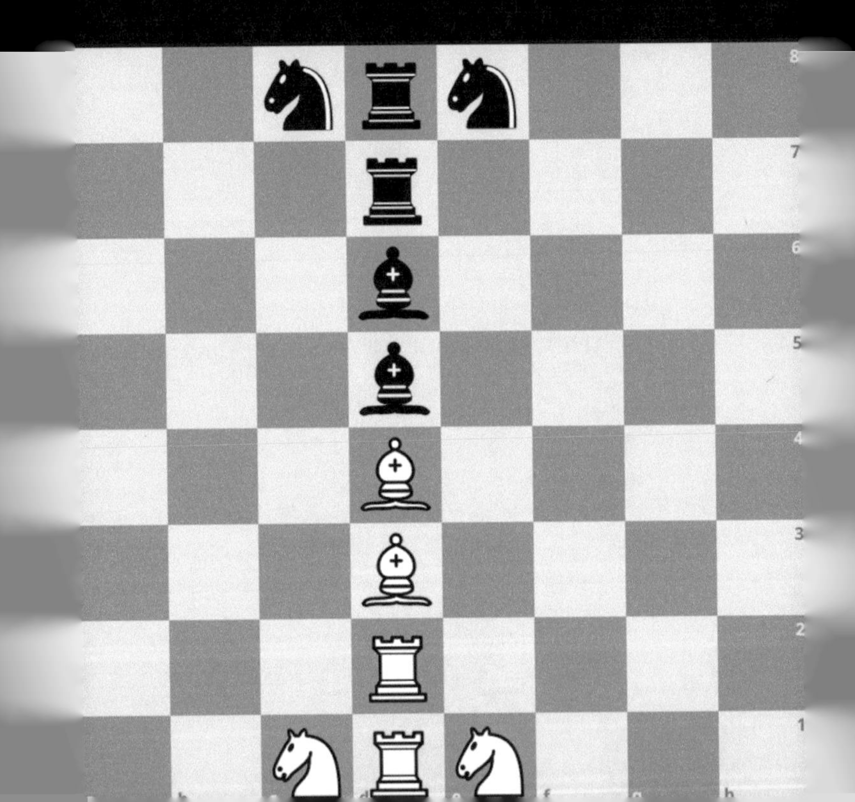

Pieces

- Bishop – moves diagonally and only on the same color

- Knight – moves one, two and turn one. It is the only piec
  He Captures on the squares he lands on.

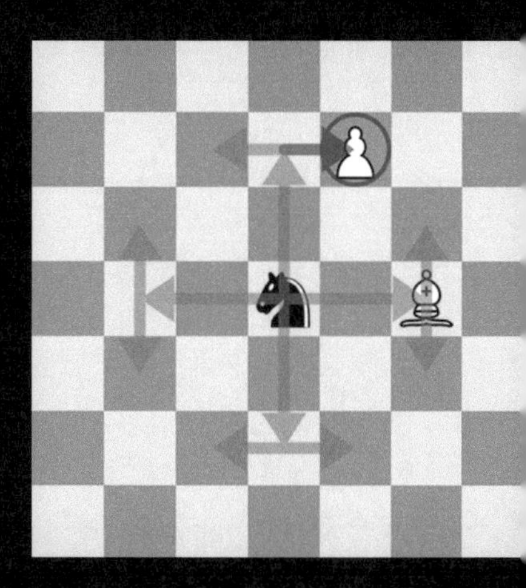

- Rook – moves always on Ranks 1-8 and on Files a-h

Gainful Captures

Unprotected

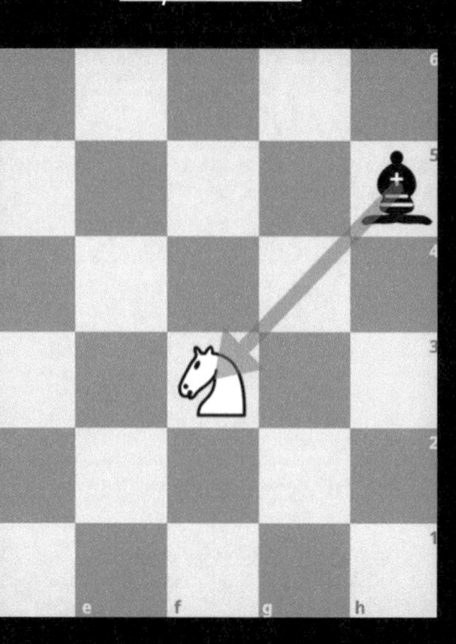

Higher Value

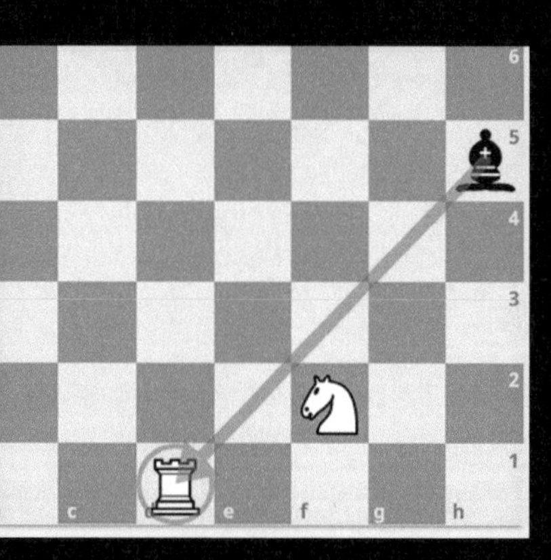

Combination

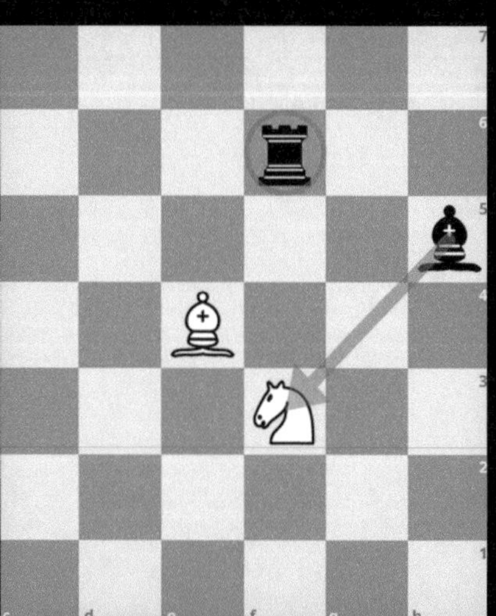

Queen & King

◈ Queen – moves like a Rook and a Bishop.

◈ King – moves one square at a time in any direction.

◈ You win the Game by putting the other King in Checkmate!

3 Chess Stages!

1) Opening – To set up for Possible Advancement & to Prevent Possible Advancement from Opponent

Launching Pad
1st Team
Prep for Battle

2) Middle Game - **Gainful Captures & Advancing for Control of King Squares**

Un-protected Pieces
Higher Value Pieces
Combination of Pieces

3) End Game **– Control of King Squares for CHECKMATE**

Control King Squares
Attack Them
Combination &
Individually

Setting up the Chess board

Kings and Queens in the Center on the back rank

Rooks are in the corners like Towers of a Castle

Knights are always riding in
and out of the Castle

Bishops are considered religion and
they are always next to K & Q

Pawns in front like a Great Wall

- Complete Set-Up –

1) Opening – to start the Game

(Control Center Squares d4, d5, e4, e5)

BLACK

1- pawn e5, 2- Bishop c5, 3- pawn d6,

4- Bishop e6, 5- Knight f6, 6- Knight c6,

7- Queen d7 or e7, 8- Castle KS or QS

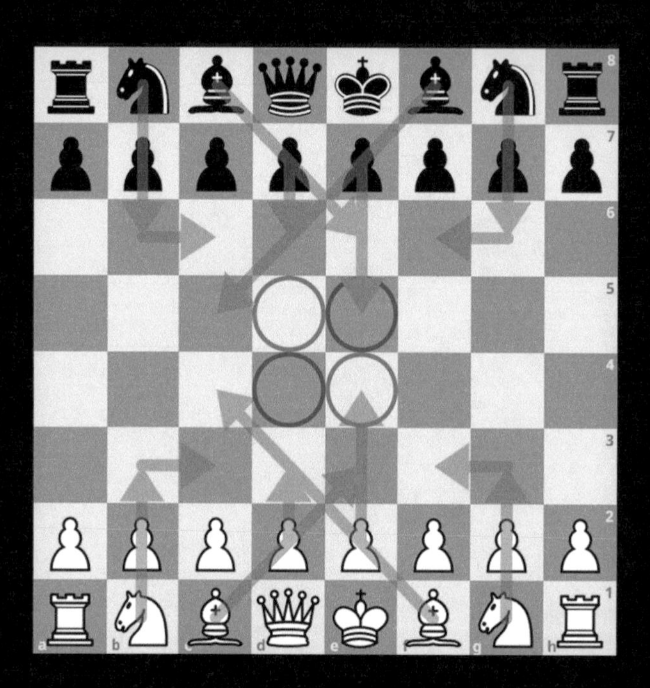

(Control Center Squares d4, d5, e4, e5)

WHITE

1- pawn e4, 2- Bishop c4, 3- pawn d3,

4- Bishop c4, 5- Knight c3, 6- Knight f3,

Opening – for Advancement & Prevention

- The Six Pieces highlighted in the Opening image are the two Center Pawns, both Bishops and both Knights.

These Pieces are brought out (developed) to work together in any order to Position themselves to occupy the squares they need to occupy which make then formidable to Advance and Protect against opponent's possible advancement simultaneously.

It Positions them to have Control of the Center. From the Center they are Strategically able to Control the Center Squares by Attacking those Center squares allowing for Advancement through Combo alliance and allowing for Protection against opponent's Advancement into your half of the board towards your King.

This is crucial in setting up a formidable Ground for Advancement for the transition of a Middle Game and against opponent's advancement. Efficiency is needed.

You might be delayed in this set-up as you may encounter Free Captures to be made causing you to leave your Ground of an Opening but only temporarily. Always return to your developed Positions to complete your Opening. Warning, do not leave your Ground for Advancement till you Opening is complete.

CASTLING – prevent advancement of Checkmate

CASTLING - is a maneuver done with the King and a Rook simultaneously. King will move two spaces towards a Rook and the Rook jumps over landing on the square next to the King.

Purpose of CASTLING:
CASTLING - is a strategic maneuver of Protecting your King to keep him from being vulnerable in any advancement from the opponent that may lead to Checkmate. He maneuvers out of the Center towards the Kingside corner and/or the Queenside corner. CASTLING - is a maneuver that helps complete the Opening stage for strategic planning to prevent being Checkmated.

CASTLING for Opening

Kingside Castle Kg1 & Queenside Castle Kc8

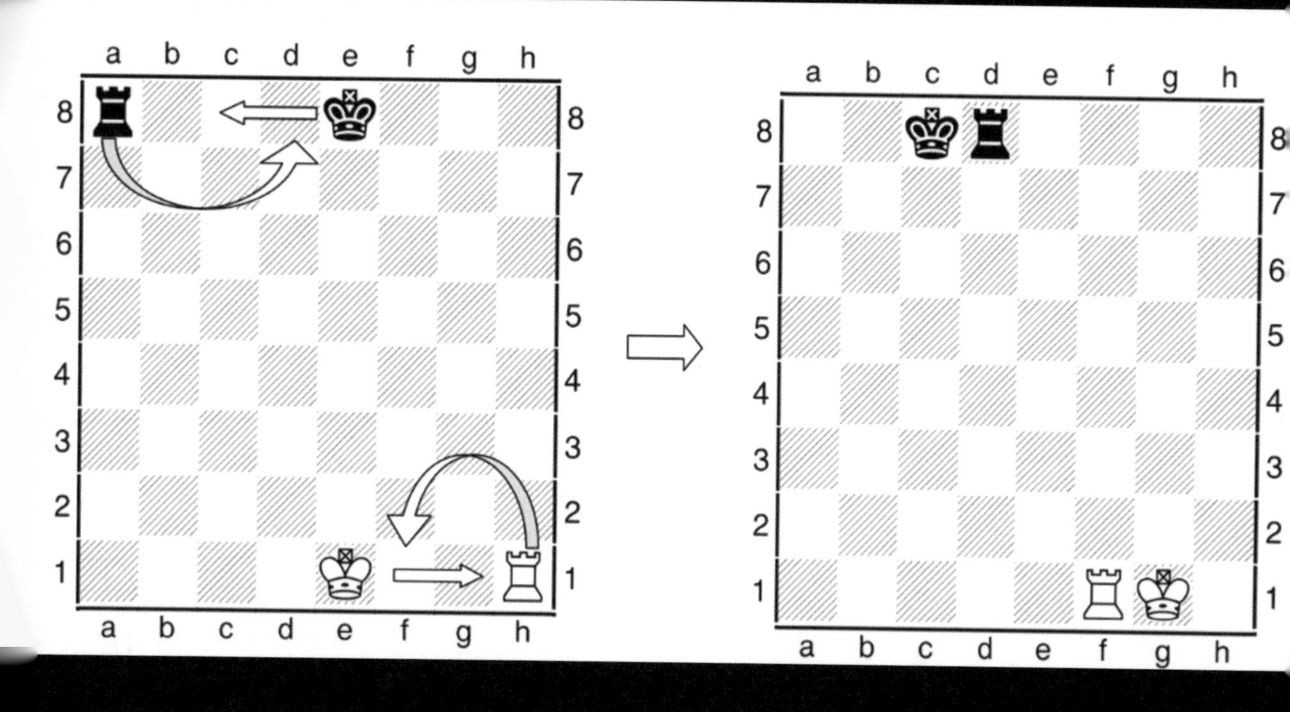

Rules to Castling

- 1-Can't Castle *into Check! f8*
- 2-Can't Castle *through Check! f1*
- 3-Can't Castle *out of Check! e1*

KING Squares - End Game Stage

Checkmate vs Stalemate

- Attack the square the King is on and squares next to him whether there are pieces on those squares or not.
- CHECKMATE – King *is under attack* and can't (CPR) escape.

- STALEMATE – King is *not under attack;* King cannot move to any of his squares and none of his team players cannot move either.

Advancement for Checkmate & Prevention of Checkmate

◈ Queen will attack the black King advancing to square f7 with the protection of the white Bishop

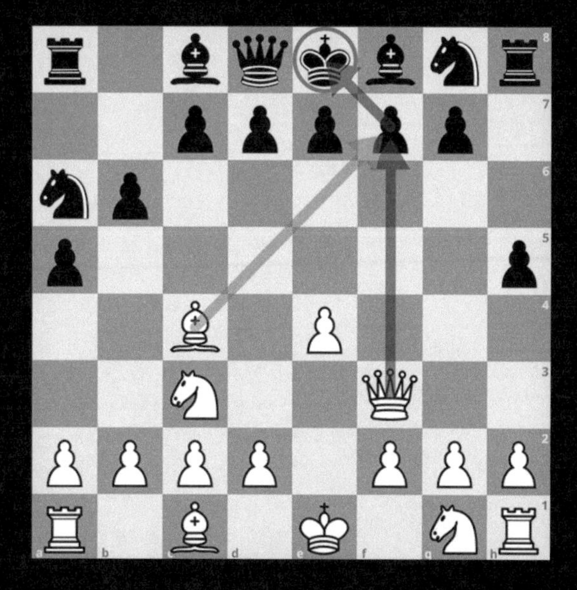

◈ Black moves to square f6 to block the advancement of the white Queen to square f7 with the help of the white Bishop to prevent the combination attack on the black King

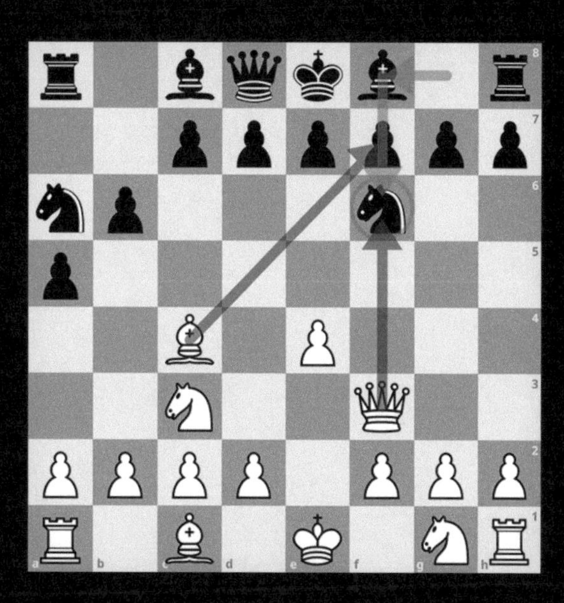

Don't let Greed distract you from doing the Math to prevent Stalemate!

It's not Stalemate yet!

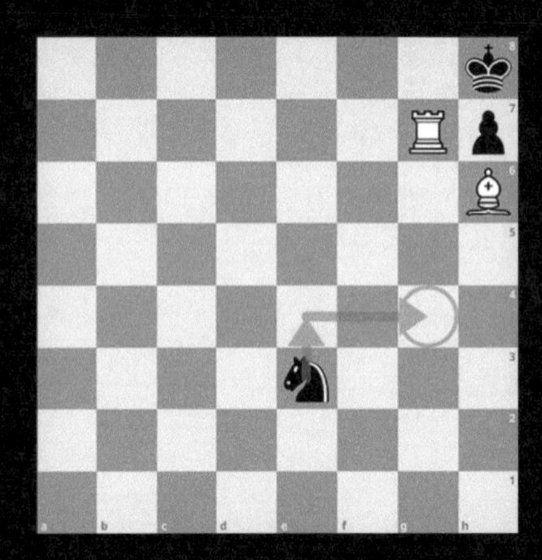

Stalemate after the Capture!

Material or Checkmate?

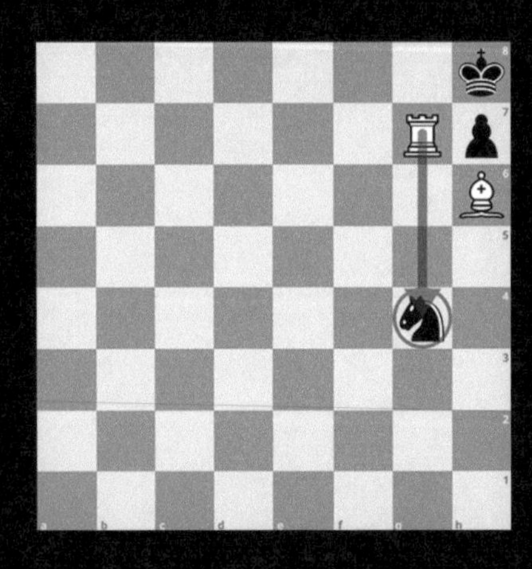

Checkmates for End Game

Queen and King Checkmate

Stack Attack Checkmate

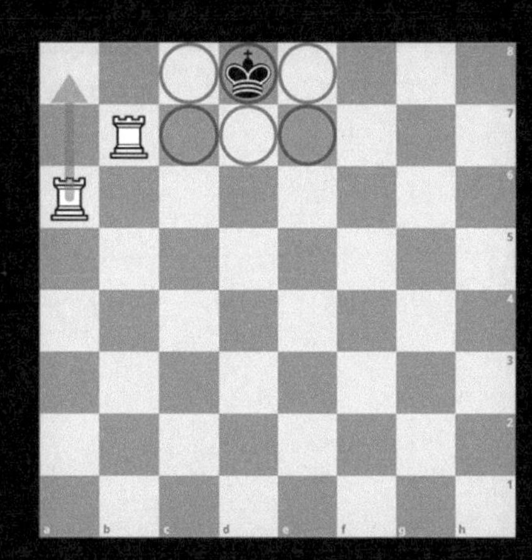

King and Rook Checkmate

TACTICS

- Tactics helps strengthen you and weakens your opponent always looking for Gainful Captures that can help you advance towards your opponent's King for Checkmate.

Combination Move (aka More or Better Attackers than Defenders) – attack a piece more times than it is defended. Better attackers is when you are attacking a Piece with a lower value Piece than the higher value Piece that is protecting.

Fork – when one Piece attacks two or more enemy Pieces at the same time. All the Pieces can Fork.

Pin – a Piece is stuck from moving because it will leave the more value Piece behind it vulnerable to Capture.

Skewer – it is like a Pin, except the higher value Piece is in front, or the pieces are of equal value for a Gainful capture possibility.

Discovery – You move your own Piece out of the way of your threatening Piece that is revealing the attack with a long-range piece behind. Simultaneously you would like to attack as well with the moving front Piece, then it acts like a Fork with two attacks at once.

Double Check – is just like a Discovery except that it is used on the opponent's King. Both Pieces, the Piece in front that is going to be moved and the piece behind will put the opponent's King in Check twice most likely for Checkmate.

Removing the Guard, Overload, and Deflecting – are ways from keeping an opponent's Piece from doing its duty. You are forcing the opponent's Piece from leaving its Protective position. This can be done by Capturing it, forcing it to Capture one of your Pieces, or chasing it away with a threat then you can Capture the Piece and/or Occupy the square it was guarding keeping you from advancement for Checkmate.

Decoying – is a special way of manipulating a Piece to go to a different square where it can be taken advantage of.

Trapping – attacking a Piece where it has no escape.

Glossary

- **Adjust** – an adjustment of one's own which can only be done on one's turn and must say "I adjust" before touching one's piece.
- **Analysis** – study of a game to help determine who is winning by examining quantity of material and their respective positions on the board.
- **Annotation** – written commentary of moves played by both players using notations ex. a1, b1, Qa2 etc.
- **Attack** – threating the capture of material.
- **Back-rank mate** – a checkmate delivered by a Rook or Queen along a back rank imprisoned by his/her own pieces (usually pawns).
- **Blunder** – a mistake on a decided move that leaves one in an awkward position where the opponent can capitalize by capturing material, losing tempo, or checkmated.
- **Calculate** – to think and plan a series of moves considering possible responses without moving the pieces first.
- **Capture** – the capturing piece occupies the square where the captured piece was except in en passant capture.
- **Castling** – a move that is done at the same time only with a King and a Rook, King moves two spaces towards the Rook and the Rook jumps over the King.
- **Check** – an attack on the King with the player announcing check.
- **Checkmate** – when the King is under attack and there is no possible escape from the attack (no capture of the attacker, no protection against the attacker, and no safe square to run to away from the attack).
- **Combination** – a sequence of moves usually involving a sacrifice to get an advantage.
- **Control** – guarding of a square preventing opponent from use of that territory.
- **Counterattack** - an attack that is responding to an attack by the opponent.
- **Development** – moving pieces from their original square to make them active.
- **Draw** – a game that ends without victory for both players.
- **En passant** – (French, "In the act of passing") any pawn leaving their home rank moving two squares in passing adjacent of the opponent's capture square can be captured by the opponent's pawn in the captured square he/she passed.
- **En prise** – a piece that is hanging and can be taken for free.

- **Exchange** - when both sides are swapping or trading pieces.
- **Fianchetto** – developing a Bishop for White to b2 or g2 and for Black to b7 or g7.
- **File** – a column on the board that is vertical (like elevators a – h).
- **Grandmaster** – the highest chess title a player can achieve.
- **Hanging** – a piece that is unprotected and be captured freely like en-prise.
- **Illegal move** – a move that is not allowed and must be corrected.
- **Isolated pawn** – a pawn with no pawn of the same color adjacent.
- **Master** – a strong chess player usually with a rating of 2200.
- **Material** – player's pieces and pawns on the board.
- **Open file** – a file where there are no pawns.
- **Passed pawn** – a pawn that has no pawn of the opposite color on the same file or adjacent to it.
- **Perpetual check** – when a player puts the opponent in a repeated check which becomes a Draw.
- **Promotion** – advancing a pawn to the last rank can be transformed to a Queen, Rook, Bishop, or Knight.
- **Rank** – a row on the board that are numbered 1 – 8 (like floors), White goes up the ranks and Black goes down the ranks.
- **Simul** – short for when a player plays multiple players simultaneously.
- **Stalemate** – when the King is not in check and the player has no legal moves to make.
- **Tactics** – calculated moves that are meticulously played for material and checkmate.
- **Tempo** – is a unit of time that can be used productively.
- **Touch-move rule** – when a player touches a piece, that piece must be moved unless it is illegal to move. When a player touches an opponent's piece to capture, and it is legal it must be captured.
- **Theory** – a system of ideas and observations that are related to each other to justify the decision of the move selected.
- **Zugzwang** – when a player is forced to move to a square they don't want to move to.